SPOTLIGHT ON THE AMERICAN INDIANS OF CALIFORNIA

THE MODOC

FRANCINE TOPACIO

NEW YORK

Published in 2018 by The Rosen Publishing Group, Inc.
29 East 21st Street, New York, NY 10010

Editor: Elizabeth Krajnik
Book Design: Michael Flynn
Interior Layout: Tanya Dellaccio

Photo Credits: Cover David Bacon/Alamy; p. 5 Michele D'Amico supersky77/Moment Open/Getty Images; pp. 6, 7 Buyenlarge/Archive Photos/Getty Images; p. 9 Bettmann/Getty Images; p. 11 Courtesy of the Library of Congress; p. 12 DAVID MCNEW/AFP/Getty Images; p. 13 DEA/G. DAGLI ORTI/De Agostini/Getty Images; p. 15 Library of Congress/Corbis Historical/Getty Images; p. 16 Stefan Malloch/Shutterstock.com; p. 17 Danita Delimont/Gallo Images/Getty Images; pp. 19, 27 Historical/Corbis Historical/Getty Images; p. 21 Alan Kearney/Stockbyte/Getty Images; p. 23 Underwood Archives/Archive Photos/Getty Images; p. 25 Hulton Archive/Getty Images; p. 28 De Agostini/Biblioteca Ambrosiana/De Agostini Picture Library/Getty Images; p. 29 Marilyn Angel Wynn/Nativesotck/Getty Images.

Cataloging-in-Publication Data

Names: Topacio, Francine.
Title: The Modoc / Francine Topacio.
Description: New York : PowerKids Press, 2018. | Series: Spotlight on the American indians of California | Includes index.
Identifiers: ISBN 9781508162919 (pbk.) | ISBN 9781538324707 (library bound) | ISBN 9781508162964 (6 pack)
Subjects: LCSH: Modoc Indians--Juvenile literature. | Indians of North America--Oregon--Juvenile literature. | Indians of North America--California--Juvenile literature.
Classification: LCC E99.M7 T67 2018 | DDC 979.400'97412--dc23

Manufactured in China

CPSIA Compliance Information: Batch #BW18PK For further information contact Rosen Publishing, New York, New York at 1-800-237-9932.

CONTENTS

CHAPTER ONE

WHO ARE THE MODOC?

The Modoc are a group of American Indians that lived in the region crossing what is now the border of northeast California and central southern Oregon. Like people from other groups of American Indians, the Modoc's **ancestors** likely crossed a land bridge between Asia and North America between 40,000 and 13,000 years ago. The **descendants** of these people settled in the Modoc's territory around 6,000 to 4,000 years ago.

Researchers still have many unanswered questions about the Modoc because there have been few **excavations** of their lands. However, **archaeologists** think the Modoc probably weren't the first people to settle in their region. Some American Indian groups have challenged this evidence, stating that their ancestors have always lived in those lands. Archaeologists and researchers aren't sure if the Modoc settled peacefully or fought with their neighbors.

The region in which the Modoc lived is known for experiencing great changes in temperature throughout the year.

CHAPTER TWO

MOVING WITH THE SEASONS

The region in which the Modoc lived prior to European contact is known for its rugged land, extreme weather, and plentiful water. The Modoc didn't grow crops, likely because the resources in the area were abundant.

The Modoc had two kinds of villages. Their permanent homes were located along major waterways and lakes. During the warmer seasons, most of the people lived in temporary settlements made up of huts. These

GOOSE LAKE, MODOC COUNTY, CALIFORNIA, AND LAKE COUNTY, OREGON

People from the outside had to get permission to use the Modoc's village lands. If someone was found in the region without permission, he or she was viewed as a thief and might be attacked or killed.

villages were moved to different hunting and gathering areas to find wild food.

The changing seasons saw the Modoc move from one abundant food resource to the next. In spring, the Modoc fished in the lakes and rivers. Summers were a time of hunting in the mountains. During the fall, the Modoc spent much of their time gathering plants to use as food and to create useful items. In the winter months, the Modoc returned to their permanent villages.

CHAPTER THREE

MODOC HOMES

The Modoc built two types of houses. The winter homes were built inside pits that measured 3 to 4 feet (0.9 to 1.2 m) deep. They had round floor plans, and the walls were made of thick wooden planks. The roof beams supported a layer of grass and the entire structure was covered with earth.

The entranceway to the home was a round hole in the roof. In order to come into the house, you had to climb down a pole-like ladder. The roof entrance allowed sunlight to enter and smoke from cooking and heating fires to escape. Most of the homes measured between 10 and 20 feet (3 to 6.1 m) across.

The Modoc's second type of home had a rectangular or oval floor plan and was made out of willow poles and brush or reeds. These homes were part of their temporary villages.

Most of the Modoc communities built sweathouses similar to the one pictured here built by the Crow people of Montana. The houses were built inside shallow pits. They were dome shaped and covered with mud, reed mats, or skins.

CHAPTER FOUR

NATURE'S FOOD

The Modoc were hunters and gatherers. This means they found everything they needed, from food to tools, in nature. Unlike many other groups of American Indians, the Modoc did not grow crops.

Modoc territory was full of resources. The water was filled with animals such as fish and beavers, the air was filled with different kinds of birds, and the land had many predators and their prey.

The plants of the Modoc territory also provided important resources. The Modoc used reeds and other plants to make dozens of different kinds of items, including boats, housing, food, and clothing.

Plants from the shorelines and streams also provided the Modoc with a source of food. Throughout the land there were many kinds of flavorful wild fruits.

The Modoc may have used plants like the ones pictured here in Lava Beds National Monument in northeastern California to make different useful items.

CHAPTER FIVE

PREPARING FOODS

The Modoc prepared food in a number of ways. They ground some of their food into flour using a special volcanic stone that looked like a bowl. This device is called a metate. They would add water to these different flours to make soup or flat cakes.

The Modoc used tightly woven baskets to

The Modoc used metates like the one pictured here to grind delicate foods to make flour.

The Modoc might have used a similar method as the Taino people, pictured here, to smoke their fish and game.

prepare liquid foods such as stews and soups. The cooks heated small stones that were then mixed with the food inside a basket to cook it. Other small items could be heated by placing them on the stones that surrounded a fire pit.

The Modoc also cooked food in earthen ovens. They wrapped food in leaves, placed it in a pit that had been heated by a fire, and covered it with rocks or soil. However, most of their fish and meat was preserved by smoking.

CHAPTER SIX

MODOC FASHION

The clothing the Modoc wore had to protect them from the extremes in weather common in Northern California. Men and women had shirts, moccasins, and many different kinds of belts. The women wore skirts and several types of longer gowns. When the winter came, blankets, capes, and heavy robes were popular.

Most Modoc had clothes made from deerskin. Wealthy Modoc wore clothes made from more valuable skins, such as elk, bobcat, and mountain lion. Poor Modoc wore clothes made from less desirable rabbit or bird skins. Everyone wore lighter clothing made from reeds in the warmer summer months.

Like most other American Indians, both Modoc men and women wore jewelry. Modoc jewelry was part of the natives' everyday clothing. They wore beads, necklaces, bracelets, and earrings. This jewelry was made from seashells, bones, feathers, and wood.

CHAPTER SEVEN

CRAFTING ART AND TOOLS

The Modoc made art and tools from things they found in nature. The Modoc men usually made stone tools. They often created these by chipping away at the stone. Obsidian, an especially sharp kind of volcanic glass, was found in the region. The natives created tools including arrowheads, drills, spearheads, scrapers, and knives from this glass.

OBSIDIAN ARROWHEAD

The Modoc were skilled boat builders. They created canoes called *vunsh* by digging out the center of logs. They also created boats called *vunshaga* by tying together thick bundles of reeds.

The Modoc women made baskets from reeds and other plants. These materials were also used to make bowls, trays, boxes, and fans.

Reeds were one of the most important types of raw material. They were used to make mats, house coverings, moccasins, leggings, cradles, and blankets.

Materials from animals were used to create bows, bedding, bags, and rattles. The Modoc used human and animal hair to make cords. They tied deer hooves together to create rattles.

CHAPTER EIGHT

SOCIAL STRUCTURE AND GOVERNMENT

In Modoc society, people were assigned to a group based on whether they were male or female, where they lived, their wealth, their age, and who their parents were.

The family was the smallest social group. The oldest male was usually placed in charge of his relatives. The men took most of the responsibility for bringing in the larger game and fish. The women and children worked hard to gather plants and smaller animals.

One or more Modoc families formed a village. Every village had a leader, or chief, called a *lagi*. This title was usually inherited from his father. Sometimes doctors or religious leaders became *lagi*. Most chiefs came from wealthy families. Chiefs settled fights and disagreements between families or individuals. Most chiefs were helped by a council of advisors made up of the older people of the community.

After the Europeans arrived, Modoc villagers sometimes married white people. Pictured here are Winema Riddle (center) and her husband, Frank (on her left). An Indian agent stands to her right and four Modoc women sit in front.

CHAPTER NINE

RELIGIOUS BELIEFS

The Modoc had their own **unique** religion. Community elders passed on religious knowledge to younger members of the community. They taught the people everything they needed to know about their religion and what it took to be a good person. Elders also taught the people that many of the things they saw in the world around them had spirits.

Community members were expected to participate in and complete many public and private **rituals**. As an individual grew older, they celebrated many special rituals. Every young person enjoyed a ceremony when becoming an adult. The Modoc also had **extravagant** weddings.

The end of a person's life was marked by a very detailed funeral when the body was burned. The Modoc believed a person's spirit went off to *no-lisg-ni*, a place that existed beyond the mountains to the west.

Some experts believe that the Modoc created pictographs, or images painted on rock, and petroglyphs, or images scratched into rock, during rituals

CHAPTER TEN

THE EUROPEANS ARRIVE

In 1542, Europeans first reached the coastline of present-day Northern California. In the years following, they began exploring farther inland. By 1650, Spain and England claimed parts of the West Coast. At that time, however, they didn't choose to colonize the region.

The Europeans brought diseases to which the Modoc had no immunity. It is likely that many Modoc died from diseases such as measles and smallpox, which killed up to 90 percent of the American Indian population across North America.

Starting about 1820, fur traders and trappers were the first foreigners to actually explore the Modoc region. Soon after arriving, they realized that the region didn't have the animals they were looking for, so they didn't pay much attention to it. However, they did bring items that came to play an important part in Modoc life—glass beads.

In 1542, Juan Rodríguez Cabrillo, pictured here, traveled from the Mexican port of Navidad to San Diego Bay and Monterey Bay, California. He is often credited with being the first European explorer to navigate the coast of California.

CHAPTER ELEVEN

THE CALIFORNIA GOLD RUSH

In 1848, the American West changed forever. The discovery of gold near Sacramento, California, brought tens of thousands of foreigners into California. The newcomers' search for precious metal quickly reached Modoc territory. To the miners, the natives were simply an enemy to be killed or pushed away. They hated the Modoc even though the natives had done nothing to them. During the next 50 years, the Modoc people were thrown into a time of horror. The discovery of gold that made some men millionaires **devastated** the native peoples.

The miners soon established camps and towns in the territory to the west of the Modoc region. Settlers immediately began to slaughter the American Indians who lived close to their dig sites. In 1849, the miners created a trail that passed right through the center of the Modoc region.

Gold rushers like the ones pictured here often hunted animals without the Modoc's permission or drove animals away from Modoc country. The newcomers **justified** their actions by saying the Modoc and other natives had no rights and weren't really human beings.

CHAPTER TWELVE

VIOLENCE ERUPTS

From early on, the Modoc weren't interested in reaching a peace agreement with the newcomers. Some of the Modoc turned to violence. In 1852, an entire wagon train with 65 settlers was **ambushed** by the Modoc. Everyone in the party was killed. The settlers named the site of the ambush Bloody Point.

After years of fighting, the Modoc were forced to move to a **reservation**. They kept returning to their old homeland and were forced back to the reservation in southern Oregon again and again.

In 1872, the U.S. government rejected Modoc demands to live near their old villages at Lost River. Army troops soon showed up to remove the natives. The village leader, who was named Kientepoos, and a number of other Modoc people escaped the government's control. Across the river, another group of Modoc fled their village on foot.

After they escaped the troops in 1872, Kientepoos, also called Captain Jack (shown here), and other Modoc people **raided** settlements for food and supplies. They killed more than 12 people in this attack. After this, the settlers hated the natives.

27

CHAPTER THIRTEEN

THE MODOC WAR

These events touched off the Modoc War. The American government expected to win the war quickly. To the government's surprise, Captain Jack proved to be an excellent fighter. During the months that followed, the Modoc leader won victory after victory even though U.S. forces outnumbered his forces.

After peace talks between the two sides, Captain

This illustration, which appeared in *Illustrated London News* on June 7, 1873, shows Modoc people attacking American soldiers in Lava Beds, California, during the Modoc War.

Captain Jack and seven other warriors were found guilty of killing Canby and another man. He and four of his warriors were hanged. Pictured here are their graves at Fort Klamath, Oregon.

Jack considered surrendering to U.S. General Edward Canby, but his followers didn't agree. On April 11, 1873, the peace talks stopped when Captain Jack killed Canby and another man. Now General Jefferson C. Davis wanted to destroy all the native fighters. The natives soon realized that they would never win the war. Captain Jack surrendered on June 1, 1873.

The army spent more than $500,000 ($9,769,599 in today's dollars) on the Modoc War. A total of 83 U.S. soldiers and settlers and 17 native warriors were killed.

CHAPTER FOURTEEN

MODERN MODOC

Between 1873 and 1888, a small number of Modoc lived on the Klamath Reservation in Oregon and a larger number of Modoc lived on the Quapaw Indian Reservation in Oklahoma. In 1888, the U.S. government gave the Modoc Nation 4,000 acres (1,619 ha) of land in Oklahoma. This became the official Modoc Reservation. In 1909, the Modoc were given the choice of staying there or going back to the Klamath Reservation. Some stayed and some returned.

Although the Modoc suffered greatly for many years, their spirit has survived. In 2006, there were about 200 Modoc living on tribal lands in Oklahoma. Many other individuals who have Modoc ancestors live in parts of southern Oregon and Northern California. Today, more than 3,700 members belong to the Klamath tribes in Oregon, which includes the Klamath, the Modoc, and the Yahooskin.

GLOSSARY

ambush (AM-bush) To attack by surprise from a hidden place, or a surprise attack.

ancestor (AN-ses-tuhr) Someone in your family who lived long before you.

archaeologist (ar-kee-AH-luh-jist) Someone who studies the tools and other objects left behind by ancient people.

descendant (dih-SEN-dent) Someone related to a person or a group of people who lived at an earlier time.

devastate (DEH-vuh-stayt) To destroy much or most of something or to cause emotional suffering.

excavation (ehk-skuh-VAY-shun) The process of uncovering something by removing the earth that covers it.

extravagant (ik-STRA-vuh-guhnt) More than is usual, necessary, or proper; or very fancy.

justify (JUH-stuh-fy) To provide a good reason for something.

raid (RAYD) A surprise attack by an enemy.

reservation (reh-zuhr-VAY-shun) Land set aside by the government for specific American Indian nations to live on.

ritual (RIH-choo-uhl) A religious ceremony, especially one consisting of a series of actions performed in a certain order.

unique (yoo-NEEK) Special or different from anything else.

INDEX

PRIMARY SOURCE LIST

Page 11
Lava Beds National Monument. Photograph. Created by Carol M. Highsmith. 2012. Now kept at the Library of Congress Prints and Photographs Division Washington, D.C.

Page 15
Wife of Modoc Henry. Photograph. Created by Edward S. Curtis. 1923. Now kept at the Library of Congress Prints and Photographs Division Washington, D.C.

Page 21
Petroglyphs on boulders at the Picture Rock Pass Petroglyphs Site in Lake County, Oregon. Photograph by Alan Kearney.

WEBSITES

Due to the changing nature of Internet links, PowerKids Press has developed an online list of websites related to the subject of this book. This site is updated regularly. Please use this link to access the list: www.powerkidslinks.com/saic/modoc